PAPER, COTTON, LEATHER

PAPER COTTON LEATHER

POEMS

JENNY SADRE-ORAFAI

for seth —
what an honor it was
to be your professor.
thank you for always
having such smart things
to say & for always
being supportive. it
means so incredibly much
to me —
13 Sept. 2014

Press 53

Winston-Salem

Press 53, LLC
PO Box 30314
Winston-Salem, NC 27130

First Edition

A TOM LOMBARDO POETRY SELECTION

Cover design by Kevin Morgan Watson

Cover art, "A Desert Landscape, January 2013,"
Copyright © 2013 by Matt Kayden,
used by permission of the artist.

Author photo by Laura Vela

Printed on acid-free paper
ISBN 978-1-941209-10-3

for my parents and for my sister, of course

ACKNOWLEDGMENTS

The author wishes to thank the editors and publishers of the following publications, in which some of the poems in this collection first appeared, sometimes under different titles and in earlier versions:

Avoid Disaster, The Binnacle, Boxcar Poetry Review, Caesura, Dash Literary Journal, Four and Twenty, Frigg, Gargoyle, H_NGM_N, Literary Mama, Mount Hope, The Nepotist, Ouroboros Review, Plainsongs, Red River Review, Sixth Finch, Slant, Southern Light: Twelve Contemporary Southern Poets, The Southern Poetry Anthology Volume V: Georgia, Spider Vein Impasto, Verse Libre Quarterly, Weed Over Flower, and *Wicked Alice.*

PAPER, COTTON, LEATHER

I

II

III

INTRODUCTION

by Tom Lombardo, Poetry Series Editor

A very good friend of mine once asked me, on the eve of his proposal to a woman he loved, "How do you know you're in a good marriage?"

As his only married friend, I knew that no marriage works all the time and off-handedly counseled: "If you're happy 51% of the time, you're good."

Jenny Sadre-Orafai's collection *Paper, Cotton, Leather* takes her narrator on a 50-poem excursion of discovery along that demarcation of marital happiness and toward a path of action when she realizes she's well below that line. How long does it take to comprehend fully her unfortunate situation, what comes next emotionally, and how steep is her learning curve?

In the uncertain state of marriage in our Western culture, where half of marriages end in divorce, too many of us know too soon we've made an awful mistake. The wedding industry places newly married couples behind a large block of inertia with the raised expectations of not only the newlyweds, but also their families and friends and all that money, time, and effort spent getting to Wedding Day. After three anniversaries—Paper, Cotton, Leather—the pressure may be too strong to answer the question: Dare I stay for Fruit and Wood? Or Iron?

Ms. Sadre-Orafai examines her narrator's sense of betrayal, anger, guilt, doubt, and follows her through to resolution, regret, recovery. There may be hope for the future, but the labyrinth must be negotiated with that block of inertia on her back, as the poem "Record" hints:

It's polite to record what we get each year.
Paper, cotton, leather.

The years measure, interpret
these gifts that do nothing but soak space.

If, instead, the gifts are pain, confusion, lethargy,
what's next? Ms. Sadre-Orafai informs her readers that
"The history of an uncivilized / romance you call a
myth."

The myths of this narrator's marriage seem like
the mythical relationships of the gods and goddesses
of antiquity.

> ...an argument
> starter. Like: he makes more money than I.
> Like: if this isn't my thong, whose hips
> were thrust into it?
> > (from "At Will")

With this Herculean result:

> You throw your love around
> and things come of it that need
> burping and feeding and stowing.
> > (from "Lures")

How much pain will a woman—wandering in
the wilderness where "there are no safety devices...
only surrender invisible"—endure in order to save a
new marriage before she finally understands that it's
hopeless?

> Nine arrows, like rays,
> punctuate this already wounded body.

It's not like you only sent one my way and missed.
This was deliberate. All nine shots received.

...My ears pricked,
poised for that sound of small wood singing air.

...I was shot nine times only
because I let you. I took each of them...
See my gentle face looking to you?
                (from "The Wounded Deer Speaks")

In *Paper, Cotton, Leather*, the anguish is explored
deeply as it leads to recognition of the inevitable.
But it is not without regret.

Fingers leave
spaces...
sighs around
her ring finger...
She shakes
her left hand
like a spider fanged
into this finger once
protected by gold.
        (from "Residual Haunting")

The poems of *Paper, Cotton, Leather* are lyrical
and highly metaphoric, populated by strong
synesthetic emotions, and therein lies the pure
literary enjoyment of this collection. I hope that
you—as I—appreciate an inspiring story of how
we might confront a life-shattering event, with all
its horrifying internal shock, anger, denial, doubt,
self-loathing, and then how we might find our way,
finally, to recovery.

Some days
we want our love to be fleshly.
But some days it's transparent.
It's like gauze.
It is and isn't fragile.

I dare you to name it.
I dare you to remember
the rubble and clang.

—Olena Kalytiak Davis

Things I have loved I'm allowed to keep.

—Regina Spektor

IN OUR MEMORY

Weigh the civilized history in wind
and climate and animal
and plant and ocean and land.

The history of an uncivilized
romance you call a myth.
Someone else says legend.
No one says monumental.

You will say: we didn't have real
history before we met. I will
say: dear most sturdy,
I've never made it this far
out in the waves, this far
out in the heart. The hurt
is bearable most days.

A STUDY OF HOW MUCH

Cars wrecked on purpose and set on fire.
His hand-tailored suits ride shotgun, singed.
We've seen it in movies on TV.

We wait for the rip, the smell of tobacco,
some habit she starts not related
to him. Something he won't know.

We listen. Inappropriate lovers
in inappropriate places. A see-through office,
a loaded train, the toilet in an airplane.

We know it's almost here. We want
to put both hands on it. Stand witness.
Measure her before and after.

We stay for it. Each strand down
her back, shorn, evidence left
on the linoleum, everyone's reminder.

IT MIGHT PULL YOU UNDER

To not miss you is to splash
back a flood with one hand.
No dam is wide enough.
And, this crush of bodies
doesn't carry your sorry face.
Understand? Oh, you must
come back to take me back,
take these knees and press
your body into this bank
between breasts. Make this
foul house full. Understand.

PENANCE PAID

She punishes the body that loved—
exposes it to too much pop music,
forces it to wear a cilice and leggings,
orders it to scowl at itself in the mirror,
feeds it a diet of salt and trans fats, steady,
walks it in darkness with clenched eyes,
tells it to read all the cruel celebrity gossip,
requires it to wear severe blue eye shadow,
talks it into swallowing its tongue,
making the promise to not say his name.

RESIDUAL HAUNTING

Fingers leave
spaces,
polite
pauses,
sighs around
her ring finger.

It's too light when
she goes
for the spoon
he didn't pack.
She's stirring
natural artificial
sweetener
into black tea.

It misses
a ring,
a shield.

She shakes
her left hand
like a spider fanged
into this finger once
protected by gold
bought by a mooncalf
face.

This occurs
all the time.
It's been years and still
with the lightness,
still with the stillness,
still with a phantom
on her good hand,
making shadow.

FORTUNE

If you visited where I live now, you won't
find my books unpacked yet. Five boxes,
mountains I can't climb, slide against
the wall where someone who isn't me
would shove bar stools.

Our pictures live in a box marked
THE PAST in my parents' garage.
Shaky photos of Vegas in May, fountains spray
a naïve married couple, grow musty beside
a car that can't move without a push.

My trousseau and charcoal portraits
you drew and I never framed heap atop
old files closeted off my porch. I open the door
most days and my face stares back. I tell
its fortune. You and your bones will run away.

WHAT SHADOW

Since I never let you
carry me across
any threshold,
I think you would
know what an eclipse
of me would mean
for you, for such
a crowded sky.

DISTANT HEAT

My thunder splinters
you in three, thrashes
you fantastic, scatters
your blooms or bones
across this ground in
the dry season. Here is
what's left for anyone
who could want to root
your skinned stems,
eager apologies.

AT WILL

We tease our death out.
We glare until the sound
of the carriage comes to carry
this white-flagged passing.
In trots the undertaker carriage
drawn by no horse and no man.
It clutches it away in its excited mouth,
a mother tugging her baby back.

You could say we brought it on,
a summoning scheduled. Please be
here after six. Come to the back
for pick up. We don't want everyone
to see. If there's a death and no one
sees it, did it happen? If only the newly
dead knew they lived at all?

Neither of us runs behind the buggy's
leaf springs. We don't poke the pram.
What's dead is dead. We wouldn't want
an open casket. It would just be an argument
starter. Like: he makes more money than I.
Like: if this isn't my thong, whose hips
were thrust into it? Like: explosion.

CICATRIX

I tried planting it in a raised bed
with wood ashes and bone meal.
I tried lobbing it over a blue bridge
where I once sunk a horseshoe
charm. I tried watching it until
it vanished. I tried crowning
our dog's tail, hoping it would glide
into hands that could give it a good
polish and a finger to fit.

MY MOONCALF

I keep you around, my stain. You're a sore,
enough to keep anyone at bay. I'll feed you
scraps under the table. Chew quietly. Pretend
you're eating petals from any spilt bouquet.
You're walking the frozen river wide to home.

INSTRUCTING THE SNEAK

Keep it between your teeth.
You will find yourself in a dark room,
one light bulb reeling above your head.

Keep your nose clean.
Remember, loose lips sink ships.
Avoid the pitfall of the tangled web.

Wear snakes around your neck.
Tell the wife you've left the secretary.
Soon. Crawl into bed after she's asleep.

YOU LIVED

You shouldn't come around.
I've asked my maids to plug wax
in my ears and to braid my hair.
I lodge sumac and wild carrot,
your allergies, between the plaits.
I even braid this body, a ribbon,
around itself to keep you out.
Only, I know that I'll unravel.
I'll know that you lived.

FIRE SCAR

Floods of leaves, little lights,
just vulgar signs of spring,

a season that suffocates
this smallest smack in my chest.

I cast straw men in every corner.
They wear his cashmere sweaters,

paint-tainted pants, cowhide gloves.
They watch me bring blaze to this field.

FORGIVENESS ACT

My doppelgänger would never let this happen. She'd swap her frilled dress for your groom pants at the altar. She'd fling her fickle body into cartwheels down the flowered aisle, those hired-for-the-day instruments sighing at her back like some flimsy net she didn't hear. No one in the audience would know what comes next so they'll grip their hands to fight their own applause.

From this day forward she would remember every grocery list in her head, eat slick doughnuts only to be reminded of symmetry, let every first date feel her up in the backseat before the date, trash old tickets from movies and planes. She remembers without them.

She would take up tightrope walking to hear the bottoms of her feet slide across wire, devote practice time to cartwheels and splits, her specialties. After her first performance, she will look down to you from her glittered perch, and since she can't feel, you have and hold all the applause for her. You hoard it in a jar, your souvenir.

RECORD

It's polite to record what we get each year.
Paper, cotton, leather.

The years measure, interpret
these gifts that do nothing but soak space.

The cake agreed to keep until we're ready
to brave again. The gardenias that didn't

faint, smashed into a book, the pages curled
tight, a grab at the stalks at last.

I look after its spine, expect it to tantrum,
heave to the floor, the year we're waiting for.

PREMATURE OBITUARY

I pretend you're dead.
I don't let them say your name.
I was taught it's impolite
to talk behind a dead man's back.

I wear black four months and ten days.

I smell your clothes before
hand washing, bagging,
and then giving them away.
I don't give your mother a thing.

I pray for what's left of you.

I stack the wedding ring, all the rings
you gave me on my right hand,
my proclamation that you are no longer
with us or like us, the living, listening.

I tell myself what I tell myself
to keep from going back.

EDUCATIONS

I practice my signature
while you're at work.

You tell your mother
we tried everything.

I learn how to make
eyes at men in New York.

You keep your ring
on even during showers.

I practice saying
divorced.

SPRING TIDE

Pull the net. Fold up
the crabs, large, loose.

We have become coral
on the bottom, broken easily.

No diving. No freeing
all the stories.

It is a close thing to escape,
to right a wreck.

Everyone and everywhere
recognizes the whole fact

when it is dropped into the lap.
It hurts. It is thrown away.

VEIL

They spell her name,

synchronize their moth wings, stuttering
mouthless her two-syllable name.

Twitching in the dark, they are
athletes that want the coach to play them.

They anticipate the open face,
wait to stream into the house.

Curtaining her face, they will
be the net wrestling beats from her.

BURIAL DRESSING

You could lay me in our bed, rounding
the old mattress' corners with yellow
flowered sheets. They have been rubbed,
washed into obscure pale, a transparent
garden. You could dress me in white,
the waffled dress, a keyhole in the back.
Remember that I wore this once,
my birthday, you took me to the coffeehouse
downtown where the college kids hang out.
You could inhale all the air in the room.
You could grab my hand on the other side
of the sleeve's mouth. You could force it
out of the dress, then so flat onto the bed,
the hardest thing you would ever do.

FAILED BEARINGS

One weekend morning I mark
our woods with a trail while
you're steeping in the shower.

The trail flails and is a comet,
a centipede curled into his death.
The symmetry is a hive.

As you dry off, I tell you: *leave
behind the compass, the barometer,
the metal detector. Figure it out on your own.*

I guide you to the trail's mouth
and fire the emergency kit flare gun.
We needed the dramatic beginning.

My distress signal is a traitor,
listens to itself, pings out, diving
to bury itself in a stack of leaves.

Tapping a fingernail on my father's
stopwatch hanging from my neck,
I ache for your failure. I refuse you clues.

I await your unsafe return. Without
breakfast, I imagine you hungry and weak.
I believe you'll eat my patient display.

CUT AND SPLIT

Kindling, that's your mewl
in the living room. I've lost some
thing. You have to tell me what
has lived through more storms—
this maul or any branch you wore.

Let me begin again. He was convinced
he was a live oak, told everyone he can't
stop leaves from breaking through
his ridiculous skin. It was the roots
that trailed his way to home.
It must be what woke me up.

LURES

You throw your love around
and things come of it that need
burping and feeding and stowing.
There will be lollygagging.

I couldn't swaddle them, the smallest
flies. They tried searching our cheeks.
They wanted us to never leave.
They wanted to skin our scales.

THEORIES ARE FOG

Theories aren't truth, dearest. Theories are fog. They are
and they aren't. They wind up only to then unwind.
Still. Don't reject these. I know not one is a fixed star.

I called in sick to work at them. Placed each in a jar,
specimens of a desire diseased. I've tied them by every hind.
Theories aren't truth, dearest. Theories are fog. They are.

They're why we can't breathe in one bed in one room. Mar
anything but these. Gutting this love, I listen for the grind
still. Don't reject these. I know not one is a fixed star.

I flee from the obvious and convict smoke from a cigar
to what's left of what's left of us. For a while, it will bind.
Theories aren't truth, dearest. Theories are fog. They are

the reasons I hawk oranges along roadsides from a car.
When I pick them up, they're light as hush, nothing but rind.
Still. Don't reject these. I know not one is a fixed star.

I'll never be able to stand the solid of a fact. Like tar,
it doesn't move. I can't dress it up. I can't make this refined.
Theories aren't truth, dearest. Theories are fog. They are
still. Don't reject these. I know no one is a fixed star.

WE COULD SAY

He's a small you with fists that clutch at air,
tiny nails scratching my chin. We could
say *labor was a breeze*, so short, like it never
happened, that we didn't know the sex until
he pushed his way out. He's a small you,
you, you with inky curls wilting against a soft
head. We could say he stops crying once
you unlock the deadbolt, your swinging
suitcase pushing through the door before
your feet. We could say he knows faces now
and that he wants to push out sounds like words,
but can't quite yet, that you talk for him.

POLTERGEIST SUMMER

They said that there was no captive tail, no volta, never
a clever plot turning on itself in echoes. The first time,
we thought: a hiccup in electricity, a blip in broadcasting,
a balloon tail caught in a tower, crossing invisible waves
on a Saturday morning. Then, the bedroom door locked
on its own. You came to the door late, broke in, grabbed
my sleeping wrists, *why would you lock me out? Where's
the key?* Then, we looked to each other's mouths
while the static got louder and louder and even
at its loudest, we didn't cover our ears.

BROCADE IN THE WATER GARDEN

Their hooked lips are sewn
with the thinnest skins.
The mouths open and wait.

It seemed wrong to take
the picture. You were too close.
It seemed like a cheap move.

I stood over them. My reflection
off their slimy orange, wanting
their heads to sink.

I would say I saw before you
the stippled mouths move
toward the lens and shudder.

THE DIVE

I relearn how to press my body
against other bodies. My slick flesh
like scales, like fish tail, hums across
men's spines during afternoons.

I teach my mouth words like *sunshine*,
cupcake. The mouth, once a fist,
now can't help but smile when it wags
these out, a loud chorus learned.

My legs remember how to braid
themselves in with other legs,
hairy and sometimes freckled,
that hear the gloss of my calves.

DEAR MACHINIST

After three months, I wanted to ask,
will the fall collage be finished
before winter? Did you finally rest the wheel
into the saw? Were you careful enough?
Remember my hands that shift into bunches
instead of handshakes when anxious?
Once you set the teeth into the mouth
of your stepfather's saw, did you take
every tooth to every nail, hoping they'd
be tough enough to bite off each head?
Did you wear goggles to protect eyes
that had to light on Rothko's No. 61
before falling asleep? After grinding
through nail, did you arrange them
around the tile like fingers pointing away?

BRIGHT REVIVAL

This can't be what you want it to be.
It cannot reach its full potential. No.

This can't grow, full-fledged.
It cannot go the way you want.

It will elude you, them, and the rest.
Take my knees and accept it.

This can't rush at loud lights and fountains
that people like us pose in front of.

This isn't a picture you can carry
after all that is left is a creased picture.

FORECAST

Safety comes first. Don't merge
bank accounts. Don't buy a house.
If you must, don't put it in both
of your names. Never change
your last name. Don't have a baby.
If you must, give it your good name.
Dot the i's and cross the t's in pencil.

DOCKED WHERE YOU NEVER UNTIE THEM

Just everywhere is her mouth. Let's say
her mouth is a petal. Yours is the exhausted
bowtie that won't rest.

Go back to life, to her head making its way
against your chest in nights docked
where you never untie them.

Stay there with your hands and your mouth
and her head and her mouth and all the carefuls,
the sagged bed on the ground making bad backs.

Just everywhere is an atlas, is windows
we're watching for something to last
until the waters swallow them away.

ORISON

I can try
an open hand.

I'll place us in parentheses
like two hands, a maw.

I can hope we survive
inside there.

EXIT MAP

The rope near this wing
is only decoration,
is tethered to nothing fixed.

There are no safety devices
in place to salvage what
might wreck like a storm. No.
There's only surrender invisible.

MIGRATION LANGUAGE

Between tattoos, he tells me he draws designs
that no one will trust him to place on fleshy hipbones
or those spaces in between two shoulder blades.

He bets his friends who can run fastest
around the squat building, circling past
the dumpster where used needles and gloves go.

He talks about the best Nirvana song,
Courtney killed Kurt, and *my wife was in Seattle*
when they found his dead body.

He tells me he watches for his machine,
the shape of a metal bluebird on purpose,
to stumble onto two twig legs and fly.

WHEN YOU ARE AWAY

Strange noises from behind
shower curtains.

Neighbor children rap on
the front door.

Noisy trucks vroom to deliver
evil to our doorstep.

Phones ring, only to be picked
up to dial tones.

Shadows flicker and fade
as people return home from work.

TOWARD

My parents' bands were stolen
while they slept. At twenty,
what would be more of an omen?

And I'm telling you that my life
has been waiting around that old
home, parts of roof blown.

Thieves are coming for me.
How nice a family of rings, a made
up game, say, rolling the rings.

THE WOUNDED DEER SPEAKS

On Frida Kahlo's "The Little Deer"

I need more convincing that you didn't mean to
do this. Nine times. Nine arrows, like rays,
punctuate this already wounded body.
It's not like you only sent one my way and missed.
This was deliberate. All nine shots received.

I think you got what you were after.
I'm sure you'll blame the lightning behind me.
It startled you, like branches grasping at water.
You wanted to shoot some of it down for me?
Contain it? Gift it? Set it at my feet?

Every piercing is bleeding. You wanted to see
if blood can come from something already so hurt?
All the angles you had to take, adjusting that bow
across your dank shoulder. My ears pricked,
poised for that sound of small wood singing air.

Even though things look a little messy, it's not as bad
as it seems. It never is. I was shot nine times only
because I let you. I took each of them. I stood still
in these woods. I let you find me here?
Yes, of course, love. See my gentle face looking to you?

SUBTLE ENERGY

He's devastating what he can
fit in one grab of his hands.

Still, she wants to crowd those palms.

She's the small bird preening her chest
in his fine fist, an aerie.

She won't fracture. Elements love her.

Moons follow her shoulders. Still, he carries
her over pockets of rain smaller than feet.

She could clear them if he'd let her.

But, he doesn't want to know
all the information—she drains

batteries in watches, her energy burnable.

He picks when to open up, when his arms
are rivers. When the stubborn grip can

finally undo is when she comes up for air, lit.

RETRACT OR RECANT

This accordion love expands or exhales,
retracts or recants. It is only as much
as we allow. It squeezes out warnings
of cardboard walls closing in.

Its wheezing fills a willful tide
with dread. I turn into this gone
love. I was taught curve into the slide
when spinning on frozen road.

GROOMS

look back
so secure is what's known

when people come
there are your open

hearts flushed on stage
and what else could be
the pins

the weights
on this accurate globe
with you

CUTTING YOUR HAIR

When I was done, a ring of hair
or a halo curved your hunched
shoulders. Your broad back didn't
flinch when the scissors' legs twitched,
when I wanted to cut more than you mimed.

HAND ME DOWN

Cards we played on our honeymoon are still in the pink
suitcase you were too masculine to carry out to the black
trunk of taxi. We thought things don't change when you leave
home. There, taxis are yellow too. I left the cards you bought,

forgotten by you, in the suitcase you won't open or touch.
I kept them there, spread out, code-like, as if summoning spirits
to see what we were made of. They are sprawled amongst
slight sand and salt, a bikini I never wore, a toothbrush I bought
the day of the wedding, thinking married, bride teeth must feel

different. I saved them spread out so that when our someday
daughter unearths the suitcase for her class trip
to somewhere foreign, the cards with pictures of half-naked
women will spill out, scatter her young ankles.

NULLIPARA SONG

If it doesn't happen soon,
it just won't.

The weight of a smaller hand
fisting my pointer finger.

Toothless smiles humming through
playpen netting.

Matching wallpaper to a duck
or sailboat theme.

Spooning powder cereal to water,
making bowled meals.

With a lean, walking the weighty body
slapping against a hip always.

RUPTURE

Because she never taught me how
to ice a cake, it mutates and halves
itself, tears apart hard work.

The pink puff of artificial strawberry
delights in this rupture—its way
of proving I wasn't cut from apron
or wooden spoon.

I let it cool with paper towel overlay
to keep away fruit flies, but the cracked
cake, all choss, wins, and the pepper mill
on the stove chuckles.

NIGHT PAVING

Someone left
the night paving
sign on, lit, in traffic
when it wasn't night.

I said we should
come back at night
with cold drinks and
watch the hot push
off asphalt.

There's this other sign,
the bumpy road
and the motorcycle.
I said I can't ride
a motorcycle
on smooth roads.
You said *I can ride*
the motorcycle
like nobody's business.

We settled on pushing
our feet into the burning
road when no one was
looking but the quietest
cars in the city, across
the street in a dealership.

We didn't have time
to take one picture
of our feet there.
I don't have evidence.
But we know
our feet will collect
water on raining days.
Our feet won't leave
for nothing now.

BECAUSE WE'RE MOSTLY WATER

I know all about the supposed power
harnessed in a full moon.

That slight tug she commands
might be enough to send you back.

People act different with too much
white in a dark sky.

And I remember your porch,
my last full moon, Tuesday in October.

I remember the way her light forced
your eyes up, up, way up.

She threw herself across the porch,
across stray cats with broken meows.

She looked after her reflection
in garbage can lids left in the street.

You watched her with your mouth
open, a reeled fish or a weanling.

THEY WILL NAME YOU

If I concentrate enough you will
swallow me whole like a snake, like I am
the prey. You and your shuffling water
on all sides. You're coming from another
county where you made wood into woodpile.

I slide a gaudy ring on my left middle finger.
My father gave it to me when I was only ten.
It was too big for such small hands and still is.

And, since I've never seen another ring like
this one, I know that if they find this ring,
in a morning clearing, they will know
you tried to take me with you, but that I tasted
like an iron fist, like poison, and then like
a bronze medal going down, tamped.

WE CAN BE ANYTHING WE COULDN'T BE

Here is the sunset every painter has painted
once—the one right before movie credits.
Here is the largest love you'll ever feel
before you die. We can say it's a wave
and it comes in and takes us back out
to dying and death and endings and violins
and pianos flung in the middle of the ocean
on purpose by teenagers. We can say we played
songs in our sleep on that piano, sand fanning
around our toes, and there was no resistance
in the ocean, in our deaths. We can be anything
we couldn't be before. We're the percussion
section. We can never die since we are already
dead, since everyone knows we're prized ghosts.

AUTHOR ACKNOWLEDGMENTS

Thank you to my parents and my sister and to Nate Maldonado, my four hearts. A most special thank you to Tom Lombardo, quite possibly the best editor a poet could have the privilege to learn from. Thank you, Kevin Morgan Watson and Press 53. Thank you to my forever first reader and the person I have the best (poetry) conversations with, Komal Patel Mathew. Thank you to Rebecca Cook and Bruce Covey for their mentorship and friendship over so many years now. I am indebted to Eduardo C. Corral, Kelly Davio, Nate Pritts, and Shelley Puhak for their brilliant work and for their generosity. Thank you always to my teachers—Earl Braggs, Richard Jackson, Leon Stokesbury, and Beth Gylys. Thank you, Kristy Bowen and Leah Maines for being amazing publishers. Thank you Allison Cooper Davis, Corey Green, Letizia Guglielmo, Katherine Hyon, Kendall Klym, Aaron Levy, William Rice, Cheryl Stiles, and Ralph Wilson for listening and reading.

JENNY SADRE-ORAFAI is the author of four poetry chapbooks—*Weed Over Flower* (Finishing Line Press), *What Her Hair Says About Her* (H_NGM_N Books), *Dressing the Throat Plate* (Finishing Line Press), and *Avoid Disaster* (Dancing Girl Press). Her poetry has appeared in *H_NGM_N*, *Gargoyle*, *Rhino*, *Redivider*, *PANK*, *Mount Hope*, *Sixth Finch*, *iO: A Journal of New American Poetry*, and other journals. Her creative nonfiction has been published in *The Los Angeles Review*, *South Loop Review*, *and The Rumpus*. She co-founded and co-edits the literary journal *Josephine Quarterly*. She lives in Atlanta and is an Associate Professor of English at Kennesaw State University.

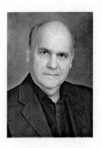

Cover artist MATTHEW J. KAYDEN studied Graphic Arts, Photography as Art, Theatre Arts, and Visual Communications at Occidental College, Los Angeles. After graduation he worked freelance in California and Hawaii. Professionally, Matthew has worked in the entertainment industry, sales, and real estate. Of his process, Matthew says, "My interest in Photography as Art rekindled with iphonography. My work is a photographic interpretation of the unique light and beauty of the California desert, the ever-changing atmospheres manipulated with apps. The same space appears dramatically different during the four seasons. I attempt to capture this, and then enhance the photo to express an interpretation of that change."

Recent Exhibitions include the La Quinta Museum, California "Creativity in the Cove." His work "Parking Lot" was selected to the final short list 50, Lumen Prize Exhibition 2012, that traveled a worldwide exhibition of digital art. Prints of Matthew's work can be purchased at Curioos.com. See more of his iphotography at Matt Kayden/ Ipernity.com and www.flickr.com/photos/ mjk2011.

CPSIA information can be obtained at www.ICGtesting.com
Printed in the USA
LVOW11s0316260814

400828LV00001B/1/P